DOWNLOAD THE AUDIOBOOK FREE!

READ THIS FIRST

To say thank you for buying my book, I would like to give you the Audiobook version 100% FREE!

Go to: www.FromDepressionsDarkness.com/freeaudiobook

Pauline Longdon

Published by Lifestyle Phoenix Publishing

A Division of Lifestyle Phoenix Group Pty Ltd

www.LifestylePhoenixPublishing.com

ISBN-13: 978-0-9871687-2-6

ISBN-10: 0-9871687-2-X

First Edition – 2012 (Print Release Restricted to 200 Numbered Copies Only)

Second Edition – 2012

Kindle Edition – 2017

Third Edition – 2017

Cover: Pauline Longdon

Text: Pauline Longdon

Edited by: Rae Brent

Font: Elephant Hiccups used under license issued by Kimberly Geswein.

Pauline Longdon

Medical Disclaimer:

This work represents the personal experience and opinions of the author and, as such should not be taken as medical or treatment advice. The reader assumes all risk for any actions taken based upon the content or comments in this book. The author bears no responsibility for omissions or errors; the text and illustrations are intended as a general commentary only, and are not to be considered comprehensive in any way. It is advised that each person seek competent and current advice from qualified health professionals.

For other "From Depression's Darkness to the Light of Life" information go to:

www.FromDepressionsDarkness.com

Dedication Page

Dedicated to all the silent sufferers

stuck in depression's darkness.

You DO matter and you ARE loved!

Find your way back to the light of life...

and kick depression's despicable butt!

Pauline Longdon

Table of Contents

Foreword by Rae Brent

I consider myself to be a strong person. But, I have to say that I had never felt more weak, helpless and useless than when Pauline was going through depression!

I could feel her pain and see her life falling apart piece by piece. And the worst part of all was… I couldn't do anything about it.

I had no idea how to help someone who thought everything they did was wrong. That they weren't even worth the breath they were breathing… All the while slowly giving up on life.

All I could do was stay close and be there, ready for if or when she needed me.

I remember when I first met Pauline in the Australian Army… She was so dynamic, vibrant and very self-confident. She was even a little bit cocky! But you needed to be in the Army otherwise you never got anywhere.

Pauline was always popular with her soldiers and well-liked by her patients. She'd always bend over backward to help people.

And I'll never forget the horrible day all that changed! The day she stopped being the carer and became the person who needed to be cared for.

Pauline tried as hard as she could to stay strong and not let anyone know anything was wrong. She had always been stoic… But there was a limit to her strength. Her spirit finally broke, and the floodgates of depression burst open!

At the time, it seemed to come out of the "blue" without warning. But looking back the warning signs were there for all to see… If only we knew what to look for. I am the first to say, I didn't know what to do or how to help her and it frightened me.

Here was one of the strongest people I had ever known lying on the ground, curled up in a ball, sobbing her heart out uncontrollably. It was almost too much for me to bear.

But what I did notice though, was the large number of people who had been her friends and colleagues, fade away into the safety of their indifference.

Once popular, now Pauline was suddenly isolated, avoided and even made fun of. Her "so called" friends and peers gave up on her. With tears streaming down her face she would often say to me "Don't be like everyone else, please don't give up on me Rae... You know I'm worth it".

The worst day came in mid-September 2005 when after the fight of her life; she was discharged from the Army and appeared to have "lost it all." She had lost her career, her dreams and her passion. It seemed she had even lost her will to live. (She told me years later that she tried to kill herself that day!)

Pauline came crashing down from the heights of achieving the rank of Major to suddenly having nothing at all. She had hit rock bottom and the secret level below that.

She had dedicated so much of her life to a cause that didn't seem to care if she now lived or died. The tragedy was, like any soldier (myself included) she would have died serving her country, and this was the way she was repaid.

So, after 14 years of loyal service, Pauline was thrown away and discarded like an insignificant piece of human rubbish. She was kicked to the curb with no farewell, no thanks for her tireless service and without any hope or direction for the future.

But fortunately, Pauline is different, and that's nowhere near the end of her story.

I have seen her rise from the ashes of her past to become a shining light for others around her. What Pauline has achieved since she discharged from the Army is astonishing.

From being a woman who could barely read or write, or sign her name on her discharge papers (from her brain being fried from depression) …to being a highly paid and in demand copywriter is a testament to her character.

Pauline is an amazing woman, and her story is truly an inspiration to those who are battling depression and those who are supporting them.

You see, I never gave up on her and yes... Pauline, you are totally worth it! I knew it then, and I know it now… And I'm glad you finally do too!

AND TO THE PERSON READING THIS...

SO ARE YOU!!!

"Read her story, feel her story and let her story move you… From Depression's Darkness to the Light of Life!"

- Rae Brent, Best Selling Author: The Money Mirror

www.TheMoneyMirrorBook.com

Pauline Longdon

A Note From The Author

T his book has been a labor of love.

As you can probably imagine, and may have experienced yourself, it's difficult enough to tell people close to you that you have depression. But, to tell the whole world… Well, there's a huge vulnerability in revealing what many people still believe is a weakness in your character.

I have always prided myself on being able to handle anything that life threw at me. But sometimes life gets the better of you… And you end up in a place you never expect you'd be.

For me, that unimaginable place was depression.

You see, in my career as a nurse, I'd lost count of how many people I'd cared for with some type of depressive disorder or mental health issue. And although I always had compassion for my patient and their situation, it was hard not to be sucked into the negativity and lack of understanding most people have for depressed people.

I believe the problem stems from the fact you can't see depression. So, you can't actually see how broken the person is.

All the big killer diseases such as Cancer, Heart Disease and Diabetes have visible signs or symptoms, or they have tests to prove the condition exists. But unfortunately for the depressed person, there are no portable devices to take a "Blood Depression Level," or scans to show how much the "Depression Mass" has spread throughout your body or how much of a "Depression Build Up" is in your blood vessels.

I know it sounds stupid… And it is meant to.

When you are depressed, people are always so willing to give you advice on how to stop being so sad and how to "just get over it." And if it were that easy, depression wouldn't exist.

Comparing sadness to depression is like comparing a head cold to a brain tumor… Yet most people do it.

I remember when I was first diagnosed with depression. I was treated through conventional methods (the 3 P's) Psychologists, Psychiatrists, and Pills!

The medical team decided to try Cognitive Behavioural Therapy (CBT) on me and give me reams of paper to read. But there was just one problem… I had lost most of my cognitive skills.

My gold fish had a longer attention span than I did. I couldn't concentrate which made reading almost impossible. And a lot of the therapy they wanted to do with me, involved me reading books to get important information.

At the time, I wished there was something simple and easy to understand that didn't take up too much brain power.

But there was nothing.

In my world, I was sinking deeper and deeper into the quicksand of depression, and I thought I was doomed never to return.

My ability to communicate with the world outside of me disappeared. I rarely spoke, and I could feel the life within me slowly dying.

Then one day, in a fit of frustration at not being able to find the words to express myself… I drew a simple picture of a little girl. She represented me and how I felt at that moment.

It worked, because finally "they" got the message. So, I drew more, and more until all I had to do was point to a drawing to show people how I felt. The lines of communication were open again.

Those simple minuscule drawings were the concept for this book. They are an easy way for the depressed person to communicate their experiences and for the people caring for them to gain valuable insight into the inner workings of how depression affects people.

It took me years to feel "comfortable" enough to share my struggle with depression.

This book was released to the world back in 2012 and marked what I believed to be the end of my battle with depression. But I still had a little bit more recovering to do.

This book despite my best efforts to "clip its wings" has found its way into the lives of people all around the world. But now is the time to let it go and get it into the hands of people who need it most. And with the changes in technology, there are no barriers.

This book is simple and quick to read for a reason. When I was in the depths of depression and needed help the most… I couldn't read.

"ALMOST THERE!" 02/05

So, I wanted to create a resource that's easy to read and understand.

You see, if you have depression, share this book with your loved ones and show them how you feel.

And if your loved one has depression, share this book with them and get them to show you how they feel.

You'll have a better understanding of where they are and what they need from you.

I honestly never thought depression would happen to me and as horrible as it was, I'm kind of glad it did. I feel I'm a better person because of it.

But I had no desire to stay depressed, it would not define me! So, after I realized that suicide was not an option, I tried many different ways to get better and eventually I found something that worked. People laughed at me back then, and they still laugh at me today when I tell them how I got better.

I am the one laughing now, and I mean in every way. And I'm happy to get my laugh lines back.

I wanted to share my journey with you so you know life can be different and be yours once again. Never give up on yourself. Know you are important… Stop listening to the voice of depression that keeps talking to you in your head.

Instead, start listening to your inner voice which is telling you everything is ok, and you will be better again soon.

It's time to kick depression's despicable butt and get your life back!

Pauline Longdon

Chief Escape Artist from Depression's Darkness

www.FromDepressionsDarkness.com

Pauline Longdon

Chapter 1: Why Me?

"Pauline, you have Major Depression!" the Doctor said to me.

"Is that supposed to be funny, because it's not?" I replied.

"I'm not sure I get what you mean?" he looked puzzled.

"Well, look at the rank on my shirt. I'm a freaking Major!" I said.

"Oh!" He gasped.

"How about this… I get demoted to Captain and get diagnosed with a smaller dose of depression, and I go back to work and what I was doing." I said.

The doctor just looked at me, and then he laughed.

"That's pretty funny!" he said.

"Not from where I'm sitting. What are people going to say?" I asked.

"Pauline, if anyone can beat this, you can. And what people say doesn't matter. Besides, people adore you! Go home and rest, I'll see you in three days." he said trying to cheer me up.

I walked out of the doctor's office with a hand full of paperwork and broken dreams. I knew how mental illness was seen in the Army. And I knew I had a fight ahead of me to keep doing what I loved… being an Army Nurse.

As I handed my paperwork to the nurse, she tried to avoid eye contact. I reassured her that she couldn't catch depression. But she said she wasn't worried about catching anything from me. She didn't want me to see the tears in her eyes.

The nurse was a friend of mine and one of my civilian staff.

She had cared for many soldiers and Officers with similar conditions. She told me that seeing me broken was heart breaking.

"But Pauline… You're so strong! And they broke you! What chance does anyone else have?" she said.

I didn't have an answer for her because I honestly didn't know how I'd ended up where I was.

My friend walked me down to the Mental Health Unit.

"They're expecting you. Well… Not really! They're in shock as well. The psychologists are arguing about who will treat you." She said

"Huh! I don't think I'm any kind of a prize to fight over." I replied

"Oh, they're not fighting to have you. They don't want you as a patient because they'll lose you as a friend!" she said with her voice breaking.

Her words and sadness felt so distant to me. It was like I was looking in on a dream. I felt disconnected and numb.

"Here she is! Hey Ma'am how are you doing?" Asked one of the staff.

"I've been better! And you can call me Pauline." I replied

"Well, we'll take great care of you, Ma'am... I mean Pauline!" he replied.

That was the start of my life as a person with a mental health condition.

Fortunately for me, they didn't think I was sick enough to be admitted. And I was relieved. I hated being treated in the hospital I worked in... Especially at my rank. I could just imagine the rumors that would already be spreading like wild fire.

I didn't want to think about it. I just wanted to go home and hide in my cocoon!

By the time I left the hospital that day, I was exhausted.

They sent me home with a bag full of drugs that were supposed to make everything better. As I drove home, the tears finally fell. I could hardly see the road.

But something did catch my eye on the drive home... A big sturdy tree!

The Slippery Slope

I walked up the stairs into my kitchen. The house was quiet and my cats were a bit puzzled at their human's unexpected arrival home. My gray cat, Storm, could sense my despair and stayed close, but not too close.

I took the bottle of medication out of the paper bag and looked at the label.

It was hard to read the writing because of the tears and my shaking hands.

I felt like an absolute failure. Why couldn't I just keep hiding it from everyone? I was doing a great job until they pushed me just that little bit further.

I opened the bottle and shook out a tablet.

As it sat in my hand, I wondered if it would help me get better. But deep down, I already knew the answer.

Being in the Army though, I had no choice. I had to take the medication if I wanted to stay in. I had to do what I was told.

I put the pill in my mouth and swallowed it with a mouthful of water. The pill wasn't large by any means, but the enormity of my situation made me gag!

Swallowing that pill was me admitting I wasn't right! There was something very wrong with me, and now there was no turning back.

That was the day my life changed forever…

Chapter 2: My Journey In Pictures

Having the time
of your life!

You feel numb and hollow

You don't know
the person in the mirror

You wish you wouldn't wake up in the morning

And even when you think you're at rock bottom...

Pauline Longdon

Everything gives way...
taking you to an
all new LOW!!!

You feel like you're

on a roller coaster

in the dark

Nothing makes you happy or joyful anymore...

Pauline Longdon

But you're not ALONE...
There are many
just like you!

Isn't always a freight train speeding towards you!!

No matter how bad things look...

Some days you'll feel a little bit better

Some days you'll feel a whole LOT better

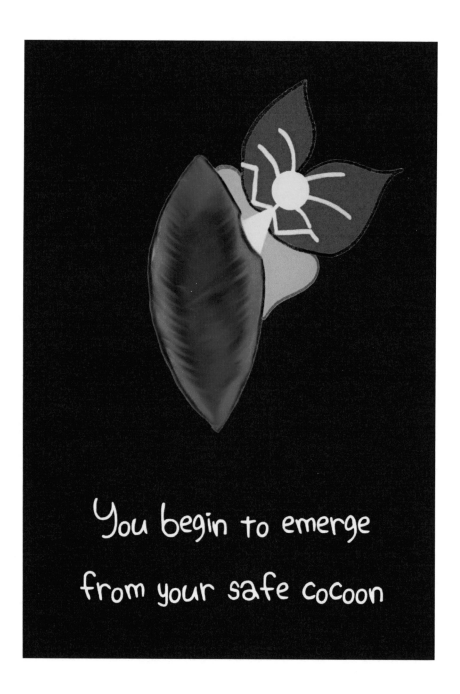

You begin to emerge
from your safe cocoon

You start to feel stronger

You just need to change the way you look at things to see it!

You'll feel like you've just fought the toughest battle of your life...

Because you have!

And you WON!!

CONGRATULATIONS!

There are many different roads to recovery...

You'll feel more enlightened from your experience

You'll be a better:
Friend, Partner,
Person and...

Pauline Longdon

Chapter 3: The Big Decision

T he day I was discharged from the Army was supposed to be my last day on the planet.

There was no farewell, no thank you, not even a card… Just a "sign here and hand your ID pass in at the gate on the way out."

It wasn't exactly the exit from the Army I imagined.

As I drove out of the Barracks for the last time, I felt my heart break, and I was filled with an overwhelming sense of despair. After almost 14 years of dedicated, loyal and selfless service… I was thrown away like a worthless piece of human rubbish!

I couldn't expect any more from them though because that's the nature of the beast. In the Army, everyone is replaceable, and my absence wouldn't upset a thing. Life would go on… For them.

But, as for me going on… I had a different plan.

I knew this day was coming and I had given my options a lot of thought. A lot of thought!

The medical team told me I'd never nurse again and that I would always be depressed. And as appealing as that sounded (dripping with sarcasm!), I thought about my other option… death.

Death didn't scare me. For me, it was a way to escape the daily torture and the future torment.

Pauline Longdon

My home was only a 20-minute drive from the Barracks, and I had to go past a sturdy tree that had always caught my eye. I had often thought how easy it would be to drive into the tree.

And on my discharge day… That was my plan.

I activated *"Operation: I've Gotta Get Outta This Place!"* And the tears flowed one last time.

When I was a few minutes away from my final destination, a funny thing happened... The tears stopped. I felt a calmness come over me and I knew I was making the right decision. There wasn't much traffic on the road, so it made the speedy, planned detour easier to achieve.

As I rounded the corner, the tree was visible in the distance. That was my signal to speed up.

My foot pushed down on the accelerator, and my car sped up. I steered my car toward the tree.

I was staring at the tree with my foot firmly planted on the accelerator... I was relieved that in a few seconds this nightmare would all be over!

"STOP YOU FUCKING IDIOT! You're going to fuck it up and be a vegetable! STOP!" a voice screamed in my head.

I snapped out of my trance and swerved away from the tree and slowed my car down. I stopped by the side of the road. I was shaking uncontrollably, and the tears started flowing again.

I was livid at being interrupted and I screamed! "What the FUCK!"

As much as I hated the intrusion of the anonymous voice, there was an element of truth. I had screwed up my life so much, so what made me think I could do my death properly?

At that moment, my stupid need for perfection stopped me. I had nursed too many people who had got it wrong and watched how they lived with the constant reminder of their actions, every day.

Just my luck, I'd suffer the same fate.

I started my car, drove home and did the only thing I could... Curl myself up into a ball and cry until I couldn't cry anymore.

By the time my partner came home from work, I was semi human again. I didn't even tell them what I had tried to do. No one had to know. It was none of their business.

So why did I even try to kill myself?

Despite having a loving partner, I didn't want to be alive anymore.

It wasn't that they weren't enough... I wasn't enough!

It wasn't that they had let me down... I had let myself down!

I wasn't the person they fell in love with.

Every breath I took could have been used better by someone else.

I was an absolute waste of space.

Everything I could do and loved to do had been taken away from me. I loved being a nurse, and I was so proud to be an Army Officer. I wore my uniform with pride.

Pauline Longdon

I was surrounded by a community of people who felt the same.

And suddenly, I was kicked out of the "club" and I had to fend for myself. I had no identity and didn't "belong" anymore.

So, I decided to move out of the way… Permanently.

If you've never been in a similar situation, that kind of thought process may not make any sense to you. Looking back at it now, it doesn't make much sense to me either. But at the time it made perfect sense.

After the realization that I'd probably be here for a while yet, I had a decision to make.

I could stay depressed and live down to the predictions of the medical team… Or I could find a way to climb out of the dark abyss of depression and get on with my life.

I chose to find a way to move out of depression's darkness into the light of life. And I'm glad I did!

I am grateful for the "bonus days" I have lived because I didn't drive into that tree. They have been some of the best days of my life!

And just for the record…

That tree is still standing proudly… And so am I.

Chapter 4: Bonus Days

N ow and then, I sit back and think about that hot September day in 2005, when I decided to drive into a tree.

It's tough to think that I decided to cash in the rest of my days, with no idea of what was yet to come.

I know I have the luxury of knowing now what I couldn't back then. And if I could reach back in time, I'd tell myself to… Stop the car!

The reality is... my journey out of depression's darkness has been a tough one.

It's been filled with struggle, disappointment, and disillusionment… But it's also had some of the most amazing days I've ever had.

I like to acknowledge my bonus birthdays.

I love to celebrate my bonus anniversaries.

I get to go on bonus trips to countries I'd never visited before 2005.

I have a bonus career that I love (and enjoy more than nursing and being an Army Officer put together!).

I have bonus friends all around the world.

I get to spend bonus time with my loved ones.

And I have even experienced the birth of my "bonus" niece.

Now, had I been successful in my desperate attempt to leave the planet on that fateful day... None of this would have happened.

And I'm so glad it has all happened... My life is much richer because of it.

It's funny though. I often have people tell me how lucky I am. They see me now, and from the outside, I'll admit things look great... And for the most part, they are. But I don't think any luck has been involved at all.

I don't think it was "lucky" to get major depression or be kicked out of the Army like a piece of human rubbish. I don't even believe it was "lucky" I didn't drive into the tree.

There's a saying "The harder I work, the luckier I am" and this sums up the secret of my success. Especially when it comes to escaping from depression's death grip!

And I had to work hard. You see, my recovery has been totally medication free. And there's a good reason for that (I'll share the story in the next chapter).

But all the hard work has been worth it.

Every bonus day I have is a precious gift. So far, I've had over 4,000, and I fully intend to have at least 20,000 more "bonus days" before I leave this planet for good.

Chapter 5: Going It Alone

T he first time I took an anti-depressant pill, I gagged. It wasn't because the pill was too big. That wasn't it! It was the feeling of failure and defeat that was the hard part to swallow.

When it came to my journey through depression, I had some strong intuitive insights. And the first happened when I took that first pill.

Deep down I felt the tablet was only going to treat the symptoms of the depression… But it wouldn't do a single thing about the cause.

But because I was in the Army, I had no choice but to follow their treatment regime… Despite any misgivings, I had about it.

The medications they gave me initially didn't have the desired effect. I became anxious and couldn't sleep (I kept seeing dead people hiding under my bed. It was terrifying! Finally, I would finally go to bed just as the sun came up. But sleep rarely came).

There was one good thing that happened because of the medication… I lost weight. But that could have happened because I wasn't eating.

The medical team struggled to get on top of the depression, so my doses were increased, and other drugs were added to the mix. But nothing they did had the effect they wanted.

Finally, they decided to put me on a medication that did what they wanted, but only at high doses.

Sleep was still a huge issue, and I went days without sleeping. So, they put me on a sleeping tablet that gave me a small window of opportunity to go to sleep… but if I missed it, I went weird and did stupid things.

The worst thing I did under the effects of that drug was to fall through a heavy glass door. Fortunately, I didn't break it, but it was knocked off its tracks. So, I got myself up, picked up the door and wobbled it back on to its tracks again. No problem! (Years later I needed to repair that same door, and I was surprised to find I couldn't lift it by myself. I had to get another person to help me, and even then, we struggled to lift it!)

At least I didn't have the complications other people had on that same drug. There were reports of people sleep walking, sleep driving and even having "sleep sex" with their neighbors… I was boring in comparison. Thank goodness! (You should have seen my neighbors!)

When I was finally taken off that sleeping medication, I was taking five a night, and it still was "hit and miss" as to whether I'd sleep or not.

I was in a living nightmare.

Not too long after being changed to the new antidepressant, I started to put on weight. But the problem was… I was hardly eating.

People thought I was sitting at home all day eating, but I barely had any food in the house (apart from cat food. My cats wouldn't handle being starved!). I hated being on that drug and wanted to get off it. But I was told to get off it; we'd have to slowly reduce the dose because the side effects were horrendous if it was done too quickly.

I was told I needed to stay on the high dose for a while longer.

Now, I can't recall how it happened, but one day I got really sick, and had to report to the Army base hospital for treatment. I'd been taking the antidepressant, but I was "all over the place."

Next thing I knew, I was admitted to the ward and placed on close watch. I had some kind of a drug reaction and it was scary. I was manic, my skin was crawling, and I was counting the flickering of the fluorescent lights in my room.

I genuinely feared for my life. I thought I was going to die!

The medical team didn't know what was going on, so all the medications were stopped abruptly! It was both a blessing and a curse.

They couldn't put me on anything else until everything settled down. I didn't have enough blood in my medication.

In that moment of mania, I decided that I would not take any more medication! That was in early 2005.

I decided to "go it alone!"

But my decision was one filled with enormous consequences... It was the end of my military career.

As the drugs worked their way out of my system, I had some truly disturbing experiences.

Many of my senses were supercharged and not in a good way.

I remember one time sitting in my psychologist's office counting how many times her old computer monitor flickered, as she droned on about something. I was painfully aware of every sound and light in the room... And it freaked me out.

Another time as I was driving, a car pulled out in front of me unexpectedly. My partner yelled to warn me… But the sound reverberated and seared through my skin as though it was made of millions of super sensitive ears with raw nerves lining the ear canal. My body contracted involuntarily, which made the driving situation worse.

I burst into hysterical tears and tried to find a place to pull off the road. The pain was so intense I can still remember it vividly, as though it happened today.

So, it's no surprise that when the psychiatrist wanted to put me back on medication… It was always met with an emphatic "NO!"

It has been incredibly difficult "going it alone," but I feel I had no other choice.

Things became easier for me after I was discharged from the Army because I could choose my own path.

I tried conventional and non-conventional methods in an attempt to beat depression. And I'm happy to say I found a few things that worked well for me. (I'll share these in a later chapter).

In fact, they worked so well, that when I submitted my claim for compensation… It was rejected!

When it comes to depression, you need to do what's right for you. Whether you use medication or meditation… It doesn't matter, as long as you get the results you want.

Depression has no right to rob you of your future. Do what you need to do to defeat it!

Chapter 6: Not Depressed Enough

"Depressed people don't have showers every day. I don't think you are as depressed as they think you are. Besides, you look too happy." Said the doctor.

I just looked at him in disbelief.

"So, you think I'm making it up?" I replied

"No, of course not. I just don't think you have depression nor had it at all," he said

"So, if I never had depression, then I was wrongfully discharged… can I have my job back?" I replied

"I don' think it works that way" he chuckled

I didn't think what I said was terribly "chuckle" worthy! He had essentially called me a liar.

This was the doctor assessing my compensation claim. And his "off the cuff" comments worried me.

I had answered his questions honestly, but he had seemed to have his own ideas on what they meant.

Take the showering daily example.

I had told him that I showered daily and apparently in his model of the world… depressed people don't shower every day.

But what he didn't take into consideration was… as a high functioning-individual and a nurse, one shower was a lot less than I was used to.

In my job in the Army, it was common for me to have up to 3 showers a day.

I would have a shower to wake myself up in the morning, go and do physical training with my unit, then have a shower before I started work on the hospital ward.

Then after working with sick people all day, I'd come home and have a shower.

Some people might think I'm a germaphobe... And they'd be right! But I never got sick and besides, it was a nice way to "wash" off the day's work and get into home mode.

So, when I told the doctor that I had one shower a day... It was less than I was used to.

And the other thing that I didn't mention was how successful the shower was.

More times than I'm comfortable admitting, my partner came home from work and asked me how my shower was. I was amazed! How did they know I'd had a shower?

So, one day I asked, and they replied, "You still have the shampoo in your hair!"

I had been sitting there all day with shampoo in my hair!

But according to that doctor... having a shower meant I wasn't depressed.

What a joke!

Anyway, I obviously impressed the doctor so much that my application for compensation was denied.

I received a letter informing me that I wouldn't get any compensation for my primary condition, the reason for my discharge from the Army!

That day was a really low point.

It wasn't about the money. It was about being "wrongfully" diagnosed and losing my military career for nothing. Again, I felt like I'd been discarded like a piece of rubbish.

I spoke to the psychiatrist about the letter, and he was infuriated. The other doctor had basically called him a liar too.

I had another big decision to make... To fight it or walk away.

After weighing up my options... I decided to walk away.

People couldn't believe that I would walk away from so much money... But all I saw was the years of fighting ahead of me and the slow disintegration of my life.

I deserved better than that! I had decided to stick around for some reason, and these jokers weren't about to ruin it for me.

So, I turned my back on the military and the pitiful way they treated me. I decided to rehabilitate myself without them and make my own way in life.

And I have!

Pauline Longdon

Chapter 7: Leftovers

I f revenge is a dish best served cold… Then depression is the leftovers that are reheated and reheated with relentless regularity!

I still have a few leftovers from my time in depression. I've spoken to many people who have lived with depression, and they have similar leftovers too.

So here are a few of the leftovers I've had and how I dealt with them.

Leftover #1: Numbness

This is a little hard to explain, but I'll do my best.

The numbness prevented me from feeling the highs of joy or happiness for quite a while. But when it came to experiencing the lows of life… I'd crash in an instant and stay there for days.

This contrast of life has been difficult to deal with at times, so I did work with professionals to address this issue specifically. Nowadays, I don't crash as quickly, and I can feel happiness and joy… for others, but not me (yet).

I look forward to the day I can be truly happy for myself again.

Leftover #2: Withdrawal

This little leftover seems to be a survival instinct. When everything became too much, I'd withdraw into the safety of my cocoon… And stay there.

It may have helped at the moment, but it would put off having to deal with the issue I was avoiding.

Sometimes though, it would be a case of overwhelm and not knowing where to start to get things done.

One of my coping strategies is to have an awareness of my "tipping point" and to try to prevent things from reaching that point.

I'd cut back on my commitments and avoid situations that I knew would overwhelm me.

I also know that things to do with the military trigger me like nothing else. So, I stay away from them as much as I can. I can't change what has happened in the past, but I can change what happens in my present and future.

It may not always be possible to avoid your triggers, so find a way to reduce the impact they have on you.

I found that when I withdraw… I'm the one who misses out and is disadvantaged.

Withdrawal is no longer my default setting.

Leftover #3: Want To Be Dead

I don't tell many people about this one, but I think it's important to share it here.

I want to make this clear… I don't want to kill myself… But there are times I'd much rather be dead. So, if something happened to me… It would be doing me a favor.

This thought used to upset me, and I didn't think anyone would understand it. But then one day as I watched an interview with Carrie Fisher, she said she felt the same way too.

I used to default to this thought at times when I crashed or felt sad. But the times I do are becoming less and less.

The reason is that I'm investing myself so much into living my life that my death would be a tremendous loss, especially to me.

So, find a reason to be alive, and you won't want to be dead for anything.

Don't settle for leftovers!

You deserve better!

Pauline Longdon

Chapter 8: Black And Blue

D epression is an abusive, sneaky little character. If it was a human, there's no way you'd ever have them in your life.

But we allow this psychopath to take up residence in our brain and abuse us from the inside out.

Every moment of every day, depression bashes you leaving you black and blue with bruises in places people can't see.

Depression is often called the "Black Dog," but I have never called it by that name. And there's a good reason.

You see, I like dogs. I'm a huge animal lover. So why would I call something as abusive as depression by an affectionate name? It doesn't make any sense!

I worked out that if I called depression the "Black Dog" then there would be no way I could ever starve it, kick it out of my life or kill it.

So, I have always refrained from calling depression anything other than what it is… depression.

I know there are agencies and organizations that use the "Black Dog" term. And I know who coined the phrase, but I have a choice to disown anything that makes depression sound less insidious than it is. So, I have.

Another thing I do, that I'm not sure if you've noticed, is I never say "my" in front of things I don't want to own. I don't associate the word "my" with depression, psychologists, psychiatrists or doctors.

Pauline Longdon

If you own it… You keep it. And I have no intention of owning depression.

Depression is a psycho killer that has taken the lives of too many people. It has stolen the future of some of my close friends and my soldiers… And it sucks!

I refuse to be a victim of this insidious illness ever again!

Depression no longer beats me until I'm black and blue.

I'm stronger and wiser now. I don't put up with that kind of abuse from anyone or anything.

And you don't need to either!

Chapter 9: Selflessness In The "Selfishness"

L et's talk about suicide.

Suicide is a tough topic to talk about. It has a lot of emotion and judgment attached to it.

Now, this chapter does not "glorify" suicide or say it's okay to take your own life.

All I can do is share my insight from my perspective. You may not agree with it, but this is my experience with it. And if this chapter helps just one person to rethink their options... Then it is 100% worth it.

I've had a few of my soldiers and friends commit suicide... And it's brutal. The feeling of confusion, loss, and helplessness that you have when you get the news a close friend has killed themselves, is overwhelming.

One of the first things people say when someone commits suicide is how senseless or selfish it was. But that's because they are looking at the situation from their own life.

The insider's view of suicide I believe is way different.

Again, I can only talk from my experience, but those "stupid" or "silly" thoughts are rational and make perfect sense at the time. The "senseless waste" is what I thought I was. And the "selfishness" felt more like selflessness.

No, I didn't think what I was about to do was in any way noble. The selflessness was because I could see how I was dragging my loved ones into a life they didn't deserve or sign up for.

My partner had fallen in love with a different person. My parents had raised a different daughter. I was no longer the person they knew. In many ways, they were already unknowingly mourning the loss of who I'd once been.

After being told I'd be depressed for the rest of my life, I felt there was only one way to spare my loved ones a lifetime of watching me slowly die… And that was to do it quickly.

I didn't even write a note. Nothing I could say would ever explain what I wanted them to know. Besides, I figured actions speak louder than words.

And I also had the added problem of communicating in the written form. I found it difficult to string a sentence together or express myself in any meaningful way.

Despite having spent years at University to get a Nursing Degree, my brain was so fried I could barely read or write. So, I decided against leaving a note.

When I look back at the state I was in as I drove my car towards that tree, I was calm and committed to ending my life. For the first time in a long time, I didn't question myself or think I was stupid. My actions made sense to me.

As you know, I was rudely interrupted by some "mystery voice," and I narrowly avoided a disaster that day. And as much as I am glad my life didn't end that day, I still understand why I made the decision I did.

The problem wasn't the Army, my partner, my parents, my friends or the world… The problem was me. And every problem has a solution.

Seeing suicide from the inside has given me more compassion for my close friends and soldiers who have taken their own lives.

Also, being subjected to a system that wears vulnerable, fragile, broken people down… I can also understand why some of my soldiers chose to kill themselves rather than continue to fight for their basic entitlements.

And out of everything… This upsets me the most!

When I was in the Army, I took great care of my soldiers. I made sure they were safe and well cared for, so they could go home to their loved ones. But then when they are broken by the same system that broke me, and discharged… They are treated so poorly that they believe the only answer is to take their own life.

I know that crushing pain because I experienced it when I had my application for compensation rejected. But I knew if I tried to fight the system… I'd become a statistic.

When these veterans killed themselves, I thought their deaths were a senseless waste… Not because they took their own life, but because their deaths were totally avoidable if only they had been cared for properly.

My heart breaks as I remember these young men and women, who survived the dangers of military life… Only to lose their life on home soil.

I'm proud to have served with them, and I will always remember them.

Important note: If you do feel suicidal, please reach out for help. There are plenty of hotlines and agencies that help people in their moment of need.

Pauline Longdon

Getting an external perspective can help you see what is invisible to you. Depression will cover your eyes and tell you, you are useless and meaningless... This is not true!

The fact is... You wouldn't be here if you weren't meant to be here. There are no accidents!

Don't let Depression, the dream stealer, steal your future from you.

You're here to do amazing things. Let's show the world what you can do.

Chapter 10: The Heaviest Burden Of All

O
ne thing that stopped me from recovering sooner was my "need" to hold onto past hurts and injustices.

It annoys me because this was one of the intuitive insights I had early in my journey… But I ignored it.

I remember the Psychiatrist I saw once asked me "So what would need to happen to the people who caused this for you to feel better?"

I looked at him and replied "Nothing! Whatever punishment they get has no bearing on my life or recovery."

He looked at me surprised, but he wasn't half as surprised as I was! I have no idea who took over my mouth… But they seemed to know a thing or two about life.

I really wish I had not only listened to that advice… I wish I'd applied it too.

Resentment is a heavy load to carry.

I resented the people who got to continue with their life and career, while mine fell apart.

I resented the people in my corps who forgot me after I'd been loyal to them and the Nursing Corps.

I resented the person who rode me like a two-cent hooker in a deliberate attempt to break me.

I resented that I was sent on back to back deployments when I was told I wouldn't be, and I spent three months on a Navy ship for no reason.

I resented I couldn't be promoted to Major because I'd been on deployment for so long, my "deployment readiness" was out of date... But I could mysteriously stay on the deployment I was on.

I resented that a person of my rank could be treated like a piece of useless rubbish.

I resented that I wasn't compensated for the only condition that caused me to be discharged.

I resented how I had to work so hard to try to reinvent myself.

I resented that I was no longer the strong person I used to be.

And due to my intuitive insight... I even resented being resentful!

As you can see... I was so full of resentment; there wasn't room for anything else.

The thing about resentment is, it's like drinking poison and hoping it will kill your enemies. The person it kills is you!

The fact is... the person who hurt you or caused you pain doesn't sit around thinking about you. They have gone on with their life.

But as much as I wanted to let go of the resentment, I couldn't. There was a deeper reason I was keeping it and it took a while to work out what it was.

It turns out the deeper reason was accountability. That's right, accountability.

Not my accountability though. The accountability of the people who had "wronged" me. I felt it was my duty to make sure they paid for what they had done.

But the truth is… That's not my job. And what if they are never held accountable? I would waste all my precious life on a worthless pursuit of "justice."

I deserved better… Much better. So, as soon as I identified this, I was finally able to let the resentments go.

Nowadays, I really don't care about any of those things I resented before.

Life has a funny way of sorting things out… So, I'll get on with my own life and leave the rest to Karma.

Pauline Longdon

Chapter 11: Quantumplation... Down The Rabbit Hole And Beyond

My journey to recover from depression lead me to some fascinating places.

I jumped down a few "rabbit holes" and what I found intrigued me.

As a military nurse, I was always pragmatic. Occasionally, I'd encounter things that challenged me… But my mind was open enough to know that not everything can be explained. And that mindset helped me look outside the box when I needed it most.

Deciding to beat depression drug free was a daunting prospect but after the horrifying "cold turkey" experience… I was adamant that I would never take another anti-depressant ever again.

It's kind of funny that when you make up your mind to do something… Opportunities start to present themselves.

This happened to me with my recovery from depression.

You see, I had a huge desire and determination to defeat depression that I was prepared to try almost anything.

That openness led me to alternative therapies that had a good effect on me.

Medical disclaimer: The information here is for information purposes only. Always consult your doctor before you start any new health care regimen. Do not stop any medication without consulting your doctor first!

Now, I'm not telling you to turn your back on modern medicine. That would be stupid and irresponsible of me. If it's working for you… That's great. And if it's not, then perhaps there is something else that will.

I found a meditation based therapy that worked by helping me to feel more grounded and connected with life.

Some people will say it was a placebo effect, and I don't really care whatever it was, because the mere fact I'm still here means it worked. I'm grateful to have found something to help me want to stay alive.

I have decided not to mention the therapies I used, because I have been out of them for so long that I can no longer vouch for their effectiveness. My suggestion is to do your own research and follow your own path of recovery. (In consultation with your doctor… even if they laugh at you!)

However, there is one particular *"Brain Chemical Balancing and Create Your Day"* meditation I did every day that helped me a lot, so I have recorded it for you, and you can download it free at: www.FromDepressionsDarkness.com/resources

Looking outside the box for a way to defeat depression opened my mind to amazing and life changing possibilities.

The day I was discharged from the Army, I could barely read or write. And today, I'm a well-paid copywriter (A person who writes ads and sales material. Like "Mad Men.") …That kind of spectacular transformation can't and won't happen in a closed mind.

I often spend time expanding my mind and doing what I call "quantumplation," which is my word for deep, limitless thought. (Copywriters often make up words.)

You've probably heard the saying "the sky is the limit" …But it's not. Beyond the sky is a space that is so vast, we only know about a fraction of it.

Your mind is the same.

It's filled to the brim with potential… Unleash it and see what you can do!

Pauline Longdon

Chapter 12: X-Rated Conversations With God

O h dear! I hate telling people about this because they may think poorly of me. But it's an important part of my story, so here goes…

Look, I'm not proud of myself, but I called God the "C" word… And it wasn't Creator!

Depression brought out the worst in me. And I'm afraid God copped it.

Now, let's pause for a second because I need to explain something… I'm not about to go "all religious" on you, so if you have a problem with God, nothing here should offend you. And if you're good with God… then I hope I don't offend you. If you don't believe in God, that's cool; the story will be for entertainment purposes only.

And if swearing offends you… I don't swear here, so it's ok.

Onwards…

In the depths of depression and despair, every night I would silently beg God for me not to wake up in the morning.

And every morning when I woke up, I'd quietly go berserk, swearing my head off because I was still alive! I used the full complement of words… And then some!

You see, waking up was a constant source of disappointment for me!

I wasn't suicidal, but I certainly wasn't invested in living either. I secretly hoped one of my cats would smother me in my sleep…

or that I would die peacefully in my sleep… But it never happened.

I hated God so much!

I was filled with so much anger it was overwhelming… But then one day I realized something important!

I was feeling angry!

Now, this was a big deal because up until then, I'd only been apathetic and depressed.

So, to feel angry was a huge breakthrough. It signalled the end of the death grip depression had on me.

I turned my anger from God to my real enemy… depression.

After that, God and I had a new relationship.

We'd often laugh about the time I called him a "C" word.

"Hey God, remember that time I called you a "C" word!"

"Yes, you have quite a mouth on you when you're angry Pauline!"

"Well, if you are the creator of everything, then you created that word too you know… and my mouth!"

"Hahahaha! You have a good point! But I am happy you called me a "C" word because at least they are useful and they are resilient… They can take a real pounding you know!"

"Oh My God… God!"

"Yes, you called! Lol"

"God, you're so funny! … I love you, God!"

"I love you too Pauline! Now get out of here you little scallywag! You've got a life to live, and you're doing a great job!"

Pauline Longdon

Chapter 13: Numb And Dumb

I did some dumb things when I was depressed. And the reason I did them was that I was so numb that I didn't think of the consequences.

Or perhaps I didn't think I'd be around to have to deal with them. But the bad news for me is… I am still here, and I deal with the consequences almost every day.

Before depression, I wasn't particularly good with money. So, when depression hit… My recklessness continued.

But added to it was the pursuit of trying to make me feel happy… and that involved impulse purchases. Fortunately for me, the shops weren't too close to me, and the Army had a policy that if you were on "sick leave," you had to stay home. So that curbed some of my spending… But not all of it.

I made some terrible errors of judgment that I am still paying for today.

Depression took away my "B.S. Detector" which made me a sitting duck for people who prey on the weak. I fell for dreamers and schemers that I would have normally called "B.S." on.

There's no point in complaining or trying to place blame. It will not change a thing.

That's why I work hard now, so I can pay off my mistakes and get on with living a great life.

If you are depressed, please be careful of people who will try to take advantage of you. They'll pretend to care about you, and flatter you… But their main concern is only for themselves. You're a cash cow to them, and they will milk you dry!

Depression can cloud your judgment. Depression doesn't last forever… But debt and bad decisions can.

Look after yourself.

Chapter 14: Tips To Kick Depression's Despicable Butt

I t took me years to find ways to escape depression's darkness.

Now some of these may seem basic… But there's a huge difference between knowing something and doing it.

Here are a few of the things I wish I knew back then because I know how much they helped me.

Some of the tips and tricks I found to be the most help are:

- Removing the word "should" from my vocabulary helped to remove the pressure I was placing on myself.

- I also stopped worrying about the "what ifs." The truth is... most of what you worry about never happens.

- Banish any word ending in "not" or its abbreviation "n't."

Our subconscious mind is unable to process the word "not." Every time we say something like "I don't want to be depressed," we are really saying "I do want to be depressed."

Say what you do want, and you will start to feel better.

- Your Life Sentence: The words "I am..." are extremely powerful.

So, whenever you say, "I am…" you own what you are saying. Saying "I am depressed" is owning your diagnosis.

However, when you use "I am…" in a positive way, it can speed your recovery. A great example is to say, "I am free from depression."

Another great trick is even when you can't feel it; say "I am in the process of being free from depression."

Change your "Life Sentence" and what you say about yourself… And you'll change your life.

- I stopped listening to the doom and gloom predictions people were all too happy to give me about my future… Or lack of one.

Start to surround yourself with people who bring out the best in you and make you feel better about life. Positive people will bring about positive change.

And the truth is… Negative people probably helped you to become depressed in the first place.

- When I was depressed, I had a lot of time on my hands, and as I started to get a bit better, I wanted to make better use of my time.

Reading was out! I tried it, and my lack of concentration would have me read the same line, over and over again.

I decided to use Depression's evil powers against itself. I tried motivational audio books, and they worked because I'd play them on repeat on a device that was not close to me. As my interest waned, I was too apathetic to go and turn off the annoying noise. So, I just sat there and "suffered" through it.

Those audio books seeped into my subconscious mind and started to change the way I thought. Slowly but surely, my mind was being fed good, wholesome, confidence building information… And it made a huge difference.

Depression's days were numbered! My mind started to realize that there was a better way to live and depression was not a part of it.

- I planted a garden. Now I didn't recognize the power of this at the time, but this simple gesture had a profound effect on my recovery.

You see, planting a garden is an investment in the future. It says to your subconscious mind that you want to see and experience the fruits of your labor.

Small palms I planted in my garden when I was depressed, are now taller than my two-story house. They do exactly what I planted them to do… Block out the nosey neighbors! The fruit trees I planted give me delicious home-grown fruit.

I'm glad I stuck around to see the garden grow into what I imagined it would be. If ever I feel down, I go and sit in my garden. It helps to ground me, but more than that, it also reminds me that everything takes time.

The palms have endured hardship caused by drought and extreme weather… Yet they never gave up and continued to grow into their potential. Nowadays, they give shade to smaller plants in the heat of summer and offer a home to an array of wildlife.

You don't need to plant a garden… Just find something that's an investment in your future. Your natural curiosity will want to find out what happens next.

I don't believe that depression can exist in a curious mind. Keep your mind curious, and depression will have no choice but to leave you alone.

- It probably took you a while to become depressed, and it may take you a while to get better. Be patient with yourself.

Be kind to yourself and celebrate your wins... No matter how small they may be. And give gratitude because what you appreciate appreciates! You'll get more of what you focus on, so only focus on the good.

I know it's hard, but it's 100% worth it!

Life is filled with good and positive things... You just need to train yourself to see them.

Chapter 15: Rising From The Ashes... The Reinvention Of Me

T he fact is... You are what you say you are.

Depression had me believing that I was worthless, a waste of breath and an absolute failure. And I blindly repeated it word for word to the world around me.

I doubted myself and my worthiness to be alive.

I won't go into the story of my discharge from the Army again (it's covered in previous chapters), but I will share with you that being told I'd never nurse again was a turning point in my life.

Because I decided not to drive into that tree and decided to stay alive, I had to work out what I wanted to be instead of a nurse.

It was tough because it was all I'd ever known... And I was good at it. I especially loved trauma nursing and helping people when they needed it most. Nursing gave me a sense of usefulness and a connection with people I couldn't get anywhere else.

So, trying to work out how I could be as useful as a nurse seemed like an exercise in futility.

All I knew was... I didn't want to work for anyone else.

I put my Army nursing skills to good use and taught first aid for a while. And I helped to teach people to become medical receptionists. I covered all the anatomy and physiology lessons. I loved it.

I dabbled with a few businesses but had no real success because I wasn't used to being my own boss. I was so used to having a chain of command and having to report to someone, that I felt lost and alone.

At the same time, I was diving head first into a healing technique that I was having great success with. It had helped me level myself out and was building my confidence.

When I was doing one of the practitioner courses, the teacher suggested that I'd make a great teacher. Up until then, the thought had never crossed my mind.

Not long afterward, I became a qualified teacher, and I even became the first Australian to become a "Master" in the modality.

I enjoyed teaching and being a practitioner, but things started to change… And not for the better. Other teachers started to spread rumors and undercut my prices (which had been set by the founder of the modality). I tried to rise above it all, but things got nasty, and I fell out of alignment (and out of favor) with the people doing the modality.

While I was building my healing business, I had an experience that pretty much forced me to learn copywriting, and I loved it. I used my new skills to promote my business, and it was a great success. But when the nastiness and games started, my business suffered.

One thing I noticed about the "so-called" spiritual/ healing industry is… It's full of sharks! These sharks preyed on kind-hearted, good-natured people. And I wanted to get as far away from the sharks as I could.

So, I decided to leave the industry and become a copywriter full time. Which is kind of hilarious because copywriting is highly competitive and full of sharks. But the sharks are easy to spot... And they don't try to convince people that they're dolphins, like the "New Age" sharks. (Orcas are my power animal... so sharks don't bother me anymore.)

I have dedicated myself to learning everything I can about the craft of copywriting. I've taken to it like a duck to water. Each year I travel to the US to be trained by some of the best copywriters on the planet.

The best part about my new career is, I have the freedom I always wanted, and I don't have to work with people I don't want to work with.

It's a far cry from what my life in the Army was like when my life was not my own.

Had I stayed in the Army, I can't even begin to imagine what my life would look like now.

Sometimes, I wonder if I should thank depression for changing my life so dramatically?

I won't lie, it's been tough at times, but I have firm goals and a wonderful vision of how I want my life to be... And that helps me through the bad times.

I was able to blast out of depression's darkness and if I can do it... Anyone can!

Pauline Longdon

Chapter 16: Overcast Moments

Hello darkness my old friend, you've come to annoy me once again.

People often ask me if I get depressed. It's a great question because from the outside my life looks rosy, and from the inside, it looks the same way… But I am human.

When I had depression, I had weeks and months of all consuming darkness… Like a total eclipse.

But what I have these days is more like an overcast moment. And I'm careful to limit them as much as I can to only being moments.

You see, I have such an immense dislike for depression that I won't allow it to steal any more time from me. I know that if I enable it to come in… It might decide to stay. And I don't have time for that!

Being the human I am, I get triggered by events or anniversaries just like anyone else, but I'm careful to be in control of my emotions, rather than allowing my emotions to control me.

Now if that sounds a bit clinical and detached, I can assure you it's not. I allow myself to feel the emotions, but I don't let myself live there. And that's what makes all the difference.

So instead of having full-blown depression… I have overcast moments that are as long as they need to be, and not a second longer.

The idea is to control the depression and not let it control you.

Pauline Longdon

It's your life!

Grab it back from the death grip depression has on it, and head back towards the light of life.

Chapter 17: An Attitude Of Gratitude

I'm incredibly grateful for my life. And I'm also grateful to depression for the blessings I've experienced.

I have so much to be grateful for and would like to thank the following:

Rae: Never has a more apt name been given to an individual. You have been a ray of light, a ray of hope and a ray of inspiration. You stood by me when others ran for their lives. You loved me and gave me a safe harbor to return to. Through the toughest of times, you were there for me and never gave up on me. I love you with every molecule of my being... To the space within the space, and beyond.

My Family: To my Mum, Dad, Danielle, and Wayne, I know it has been a tough ride for you, and I wish it could have been smoother for us all. Things were said that can never be taken back and I apologize. I appreciate your love and support even when you were afraid and didn't know what you could do to help me. I love you all so much.

My Friends Past, Present, and Future: Many have come and gone, and some are yet to arrive in my journey and if I have not mentioned you, please know you are very important to me, never forgotten, and you are always in my heart and mind. I certainly found out who my true friends were because they are the people who are still in my life today.

God: I am not a deeply religious person, but I am very spiritual. When I was in the throes of depression I had to blame someone, so God copped it all. I am eternally grateful to God for never listening to the rantings of the mad woman, who at the end of each day would beg and plead with God to end her life. And then swear at God when she woke up at the start of each new day. If God had listened to her, I would be missing all the great things which are happening now. I thank you. My life is amzing!

My Wise Guide and Mentor: This amazing elusive woman stood by me through thick and thin, reassuring me that everything would be OK. Your kindness and strength gave me the strength to carry on. Thank you for never giving up on me and helping me to find the way back to the Light. I will love you through all of time.

My Original Backers: Thank you to my original backers who made this book possible. This book was originally self-published in 2012. To get this picture rich book printed was going to cost a small fortune. But instead of giving up, I asked people to help me get my book done (this was long before the crowd funding craze). I raised enough money to have twice the amount of books printed and have been able to give the extra books to people who need them for free. Your belief in me has helped to change the lives of people all around the world. Thank you.

I wish to thank the most amazing teacher... **Depression:** Without you, I would have never experienced all I have. I appreciate the lessons and now it's time to hand me your torch... The tribe has spoken. You must leave the Island immediately.

And lastly, to all the people who have purchased this book for themselves or for someone else... I thank you! Thank you for reading about my journey. I hope it helps you with yours.

Chapter 18: No Shit Sherlock!

I 've lost count of how many times I've been told that depression is "just" repressed anger. But I've never found that advice to be helpful or to instil any hope in me.

And I love how the word "just" is thrown in to make it seem fixable.

Now I'm not here to argue with people with more letters after their names than I have. Everyone is entitled to their opinion. So let's just say they have their theories and I have my personal experience.

Whenever I hear people say "depression is caused by anger turned inwards," my mind flashes up a picture of someone trying to put a Band-Aid on a hemorrhage. Sure it may look good and even work for a brief moment… but a torrent of blood is swelling up underneath and is about to ruin your day.

So being as open minded as I am and in a desperate attempt to break free from depression's death grip, I decided to work on my "repressed anger."

But, it turns out that when you release anger… it scares people. And being angry is an exhausting state to be in.

A funny thing happened though. The more I explored the idea of unresolved anger, a simple question kept flashing into my mind… "Who are you really angry at?"

I thought it was a stupid question! Wasn't it obvious?

I was angry at the Army for making me depressed and then treating me like a piece of human rubbish. I was angry at the people who rode me until I broke. I was angry with life because it was unfair and sucked a "big one!"

But when I thought about all those people and situations, the anger wasn't anywhere as strong as I expected it to be. So I thought I was finally starting to get over my anger and was on the road to being better.

It turned out that the anger wasn't strong because my true anger was deeply rooted elsewhere. And I wasn't quite ready to see it yet.

Now at the same time as I was going through all this, I started attending a few alternative healing workshops. I learned some helpful processes and skills which helped me kick depression's butt!

One process I learned was called "digging." It's a line of questions that leads you to the single core belief that holds everything together. (Imagine a house of cards… when you remove a bottom card, all the other cards fall down too.)

I loved digging and got really good at it. I think I loved it because I could help people to find their bottom belief, then help them shift it.

But the problem I found was, unlike me, many practitioners would not go as deep as they needed to. So as a result, no one found my core belief that was locking the depression and anger in place.

So, out of frustration, I decided to "dig" on myself.

Eventually after breaking through all the B.S., I got to the root of my problem.

As it turned out, the person I was angry at was ... (drum roll please) ... Me!

And as much as I didn't want to believe it, it made perfect sense. After all, I was the person who had let it all happen... I was the person who had let me down. All the other people and situations I'd been angry at pale in comparison to the anger and rage I had towards myself.

This painful, reluctant revelation was the first powerful step towards my freedom from depression.

You know, something almost magical happened when I finally took responsibility for myself and what was happening to me. Because when I finally had the awareness that I was the person I was angry with, I knew where to focus. And when I did that, the anger shifted and even started to disappear.

Whenever I lost perspective on self-responsibility, I remembered the saying "when you point your finger at someone, there are three fingers pointing back at you."

And this served as a reminder because, as much as other people contributed to my anger (and subsequent depression)... I was the one who decided to keep it, internalise it and own it. But as I discussed in the chapter about resentment, when we carry these heavy burdens, it makes no difference to the people who "wronged' us.

So, when some "genius" tells you that depression is repressed anger... don't get angry with them. Look at your hand and see those three fingers pointing back at you, and be happy that you finally know who you are angry with.

The truth is, there's no point in being angry with yourself... so don't blame yourself!

Pauline Longdon

You did the best with what you had at the time, and now that you know better… you can do better.

So now you know who you're really angry with, it's time to… let it go!

Chapter 19: Let It Go!

(If your mind flashed to an ice queen on a frozen mountain top just then… I'm
sorry, not sorry ☺)

When you've been hurt by someone or something you
care about… forgiveness can be a hard act to do.

But why is it so hard to do? Well, because people
don't understand what forgiveness really is. And it doesn't help
when we hear people declare passionately that they will forgive,
but they will never forget. That gives us a skewed perspective on
the simple act of forgiveness.

So, in case you missed the Oprah special… let's have a quick
chat about forgiveness. In fact, I'll give you a quick "Soldier's
Five" on forgiveness. (A "Soldiers Five" is a quick brief filled
with only what you need to know to get the job done.)

To start with, forgiveness isn't…

- Condoning what happened to you
- Agreeing with what happened
- Allowing what happened to you to happen again
- Letting anyone get away with anything
- For the benefit of the person who hurt you

Forgiveness is…

- To stop feeling angry
- To stop blaming
- To stop needing payment
- To stop being a victim
- For the benefit of you!

As I've already discussed in previous chapters, the person who hurt you has moved on and doesn't think about you anymore. They are off, busily living their life, while you are stuck swimming laps in the "shit pit" of past hurts.

But reliving the past doesn't change anything. And it doesn't change your future. It just makes you a bitter and twisted individual!

Trust me I know… and I know this from personal experience.

It took me a while to work out why I couldn't forgive the people who hurt me. It turns out I was trying to keep them accountable. But I can't remember when that became my job.

And considering how much it sucked to go through it the first time… I don't know why I continued to relive it so much. Because each time I relived it, it became more deeply embedded.

But for some reason I couldn't stop it.

That was until finally salvation came when I learned a simple technique called "The Forgiveness Process."

This is how it's done…

1. Imagine the person who hurt you standing in front of you.
2. Say to them "I forgive you, I forgive you, I forgive you!"
3. Next say "I am forgiven, I am forgiven, I am forgiven!"

The beauty of this simple technique is how you don't delve into the details of the incident. You remain outside of it. And the best part of the process is, you are forgiven as well.

Any time I thought of a person or felt old emotions come up… I used this technique. Even if I needed to do it hundreds of times a day. (The more you do it, the less attached you'll feel to the person or incident.)

But me being the curious and adventurous person I am… I took this process to another level by changing the words I used.

And it worked a treat!

For example:

- To release people, say "I release you" three times and then say "I am released" three times
- To love people, say "I love you" three times and then say "I am loved" three times
- To respect people, say "I respect you" three times and then say "I am respected" three times

I'm sure you get the picture!

Of course, there are many other empowering words you can use. You are only limited by your own imagination.

I've often used this process as an "empowerment stack."

I'd go through the process with words that are relevant to the situations… words such as love/loved, forgive/forgiven, release/released, respect/respected, cherish/cherished, remember/remembered, adore/adored, hear/heard, see/seen, consider/considered… and the list goes on.

I have also done this process on depression itself.

I pictured a huge black mass in front of me and used the words release/released, free/free. It helped to get rid of the stranglehold depression had on me. (I know it sounds "woo woo" but it worked and I don't need to know why things work.)

Remember how I said in an earlier chapter that the words "I am" are powerful?

Well, I believe that it's the power of the "I am" words that makes this process work as well as it does. You end up owning some wonderfully powerful words as part of this process.

There's no way you can move forward if you are chained to the past. Use this simple technique to unlock the shackles of the past and step confidently into your amazing future.

Chapter 20: Life After A Messy Discharge... Becoming A Civilian Again

T his chapter is dedicated to all the military veterans who struggle to find a place to belong after they are discharged.

When you're in the military, regardless of the service you're in, you are surrounded by people who get you... because they are the same.

They share many of your core values and you know they'd have your back when you need it most.

It's funny to see the different services (Army, Navy, Air Force, etc) pick on each other... but as soon as someone outside of the military does the same thing, the service men and women all come together against the new enemy in common. The new enemy doesn't stand a chance!

There is a comradery that's hard to explain.

But when you are discharged and you lose your community, it leaves you feeling alone and lost.

When you are in the service, every moment of every day is accounted for. You are told what to wear, where to be and even when you can eat.

The chain of command is clear. You are never left wondering what you need to do next. Even when there's a "hurry up and wait" ...you know that you'll soon be on your way again.

Your life has purpose and you are doing what you've always wanted to do… serve your country.

People who haven't served just don't get it… but I wouldn't be too hard on them. They just have a different path to travel. Besides we can't hate on "civilians" because we are one of them.

One of the biggest issues I faced was an enormous sense of loss that presented itself as grief. But I had trouble putting a finger on what I was grieving.

It turned out I was grieving the loss of my community, but more than that, I was grieving my loss of identity.

From the moment I decided to join the Army, I knew how life looked for me. And when I was in the Army, there was a predictability and certainty. Every few years I'd be posted to a new job and location… and if I played my cards right, I'd be promoted as well.

But when I was discharged, all my predictability and certainty disappeared faster than $100 put over the bar in the Officer's Mess! I felt alone and lonely.

My chain of command was gone, my support network was gone and my life seemed to have no purpose.

Mix that emotional state with having to fight "the system" to have military related injuries recognized… my transition to being a civilian again was a nightmare.

Sadly, I've had a few of my veteran mates and ex-soldiers take their own lives because they sunk to a depth of depression they just couldn't escape. And because they were in the unfamiliar territory of trying to fit in with being a civilian again… they didn't know where to get help.

When it comes to getting help, a good idea is to program the numbers you need to call into your phone when you're in a good place, so that when you aren't, they are close at hand. Any unnecessary delays to getting the help you need could make you sink deeper in to despair.

I know there have been times when I have really struggled in thinking that my service mattered. Especially because my departure and subsequent discharge from the Army went unrecognized by people who should have cared a bit more.

If you don't hear it from anyone else, let me assure you that your service mattered! And you matter!

There is life after your military service.

Just like it took some adjustment to get used to life in the military… it will take a period of adjustment to get back into the groove of being a "civi" again!

So be patient with yourself and others around you.

One last thing I want you to know is… Your military skills are transferable into civilian life. The discipline you have will set you a part from everyone else.

When I was in the Army, I was constantly told I'd never make it on the outside and that my nursing skills weren't transferable. But that was a lie! And it was told to me by people who took delight in eroding the confidence of their subordinates.

The truth is, my skills were not only transferable… but highly desirable!

And so are yours! You just need to find a career or job that values what you have in your skills arsenal.

For some reason I believed them when I was told I'd never nurse again. Looking back, it's easy to see the lie… and it makes no sense at all. But at the time, their words gutted me.

You should only ever listen to the advice of one person… you! You know more than anyone else what you're capable of. And it's always immensely satisfying to prove people wrong.

Whatever you do, don't let the "system" wear you down until you want to give up. I have been there and I could see what was happening. That's why I decided to walk away from fighting for the compensation I was entitled to.

I knew that if I continued to fight to be compensated… it would, quite literally, be the death of me. And I have no desire to be a statistic.

Too many of my friends have taken their own lives after their messy discharge. Fortunately, there are more support agencies now that can help veterans. But you need to reach out to them. They may not be exactly what you want, but something is better than nothing.

Get your loved ones to read this book too so they can understand you.

This book even helped my dad who is a Vietnam veteran with PTSD. He had a hard time telling us how he felt and what he was going through, but when I wrote this book, he was surprised to see "his" life in picture form. He pointed at one of the pictures and said "That's exactly what my head feels like." And my mother said "Why didn't you tell me?" But he could never find the words to describe it.

That moment helped both of my parents to understand each other better.

I'm not going to lie… there will be days you miss the military.

But when you do, I want you to think about what you miss about it. Chances are you miss the community of like-minded people.

So here's my challenge to you… find another group of people you can hang out with.

Remember when you first joined the military? You didn't fit in 100% then either. So give yourself time to fit in again.

Be proud of who you are and what you've achieved.

And most of all… know that life goes on. As one chapter closes… another one opens!

Keep reading, because your story is about to get a whole lot better!

Pauline Longdon

Chapter 21: About The Author

Pauline Longdon tells people she has had an ordinary life… But that's far from the truth. Not that she is lying; she just doesn't like to make a big deal out of things.

It was this attitude that eventually got the better of her.

Sent on back to back overseas deployments with the Army in 2003, Pauline finally had to face what a big deal everything was. The double deployments took a terrible toll on her, and she had to face up to the fact she was depressed. The "happy" mask she had been hiding behind for so long had finally fallen off.

Her treatment in the Army after the diagnosis varied from one of hopeful support to avoidance and absolute disregard. In 2005, after 14 years of loyal and dedicated service, she was discharged out of the Army, without any thanks or appreciation. She just simply faded away as though she had never been there. No one cared, and most didn't even notice she was gone.

Pauline has turned this adversity into her greatest opportunity and is now an exceptional, inspiring and highly respected author, speaker, and mentor. It's a great accomplishment considering all she has endured.

Pauline is a retired Registered Nurse and Australian Army Nursing Officer, having reached the rank of Major. She now divides her time as a copywriter, mentor, business strategist, and entrepreneur.

Pauline Longdon

Her unique approach to Business, Life, Love, Manifestation, and Spirituality motivates people to think about why they believe what they believe and then empowers them to create their own reality. Her innate ability to "see" beyond the current situation and delve deeply into its cause is unrivalled and a great asset.

Pauline is an absolute living testimony of her own belief in herself and digging deep to find what works. She is passionate about empowering others to achieve their highest potential and being the change she wishes to see in the world just by living her bliss.

In Depression

Out Of Depression

Chapter 22: Resources

Here are some resources to help you on your journey...
"From Depression's Darkness to the Light of Life" has its very own website.

If you have enjoyed this book and found it useful, visit the website for more handy information about defeating depression at:

www.FromDepressionsDarkness.com

And make sure you access the free *"Brain Chemical Balancing and Create Your Day"* meditation at:

www.FromDepressionsDarkness.com/resources

Remember to download your free audio book at:

www.FromDepressionsDarkness.com/freeaudiobook

You can also connect with me on Facebook. I have a page for this book, and I'd love to get your feedback. You can find me at:

www.Facebook.com/FromDepressionsDarkness

Pauline Longdon

You can find out more about Pauline's copywriting and marketing business and read her blog at:

www.TheCopyAlchemist.com

Chapter 23: Shining The Light On Depression

The World Health Organization statistics show that 300 million people globally have depression. Depression affects all ages, all races and takes close to 800,000 lives each year.

Sadly, we often only hear about depression when it claims the life of someone famous. The aim of this book is to change the conversation by giving the world a success story to share. And then creating more of them.

I want to show that depression does not need to be the "Life Sentence" people think it is. I want people to know they can kick depression's despicable butt!

Please share this book with your friends and loved ones.

Share it with your community, share it on social media… and let's share the success stories.

Share it with these hashtags…

#FromDepressionsDarkness

#KickDepressionsButt

#IBeatDepression

#ShineTheLightOnDepression

And please leave a review on Amazon to help shine the light on depression so others may see a way out.

Thank you…

Having depression was tough…

But I was tougher!

And so are YOU!

Welcome Back!

Pauline Longdon

Create Your Own Notes

Made in the USA
Lexington, KY
01 October 2017